GUIDE

MW01114634

Communications

*Telling Your
Church's Story*

United Methodist Communications

COMMUNICATIONS

Copyright © 2012 by Cokesbury

This book is printed on acid-free paper.

ISBN 978-1-426-73634-6

Some paragraph numbers for and language in the Book of Discipline *may have changed in the 2012 revision, which was published after these Guidelines were printed. We regret any inconvenience.*

MANUFACTURED IN THE UNITED STATES OF AMERICA

Contents

Called to a Ministry of Faithfulness and Vitality

You are so important to the life of the Christian church! You have consented to join with other people of faith who, through the millennia, have sustained the church by extending God's love to others. You have been called and have committed your unique passions, gifts, and abilities to a position of leadership. This Guideline will help you understand the basic elements of that ministry within your own church and within The United Methodist Church.

Leadership in Vital Ministry

Each person is called to ministry by virtue of his or her baptism, and that ministry takes place in all aspects of daily life, both in and outside of the church. Your leadership role requires that you will be a faithful participant in the **mission of the church**, which is to partner with God to **make disciples of Jesus Christ for the transformation of the world**. You will not only engage in your area of ministry, but will also work to empower others to be in ministry as well. The vitality of your church, and the Church as a whole, depends upon the faith, abilities, and actions of all who work together for the glory of God.

Clearly then, as a pastoral leader or leader among the laity, your ministry is not just a "job," but a spiritual endeavor. You are a spiritual leader now, and others will look to you for spiritual leadership. What does this mean?

All persons who follow Jesus are called to grow spiritually through the practice of various Christian habits (or "means of grace") such as prayer, Bible study, private and corporate worship, acts of service, Christian conferencing, and so on. Jesus taught his disciples practices of spiritual growth and leadership that you will model as you guide others. As members of the congregation grow through the means of grace, they will assume their own role in ministry and help others in the same way. This is the cycle of disciple making.

The Church's Vision

While there is one mission—to make disciples of Jesus Christ—the portrait of a successful mission will differ from one congregation to the next. One of your roles is to listen deeply for the guidance and call of God in your own context. In your church, neighborhood, or greater community, what are the greatest needs? How is God calling your congregation to be in a ministry of service and witness where they are? What does vital ministry look like in the life of your congregation and its neighbors? What are the characteristics, traits, and actions that identify a person as a faithful disciple in your context?

This portrait, or vision, is formed when you and the other leaders discern together how your gifts from God come together to fulfill the will of God.

Assessing Your Efforts

We are generally good at deciding what to do, but we sometimes skip the more important first question of what we want to accomplish. Knowing your task (the mission of disciple making) and knowing what results you want (the vision of your church) are the first two steps in a vital ministry. The third step is in knowing how you will assess or measure the results of what you do and who you are (and become) because of what you do. Those measures relate directly to mission and vision, and they are more than just numbers.

One of your leadership tasks will be to take a hard look, with your team, at all the things your ministry area does or plans to do. No doubt they are good and worthy activities; the question is, *"Do these activities and experiences lead people into a mature relationship with God and a life of deeper discipleship?"* That is the business of the church, and the church needs to do what only the church can do. You may need to eliminate or alter some of what you do if it does not measure up to the standard of faithful disciple making. It will be up to your ministry team to establish the specific standards against which you compare all that you do and hope to do. (This Guideline includes further help in establishing goals, strategies, and measures for this area of ministry.)

The Mission of The United Methodist Church

Each local church is unique, yet it is a part of a *connection,* a living organism of the body of Christ. Being a connectional Church means in part that all United Methodist churches are interrelated through the structure and organization of districts, conferences, and jurisdictions in the larger "family" of the denomination. *The Book of Discipline of The United Methodist Church* describes, among other things, the ministry of all United Methodist Christians, the essence of servant ministry and leadership, how to organize and accomplish that ministry, and how our connectional structure works (see especially ¶¶126–138).

Our Church extends way beyond your doorstep; it is a global Church with both local and international presence. You are not alone. The resources of the entire denomination are intended to assist you in ministry. With this help and the partnership of God and one another, the mission continues. You are an integral part of God's church and God's plan!

(For help in addition to this Guideline and the *Book of Discipline*, see "Resources" at the end of your Guideline, www.umc.org, and the other websites listed on the inside back cover.)

Biblical Basis for Communications

Congratulations! By accepting the position of communications coordinator, you will help your congregation get important information and share the Christian message with each other and the community. It's a wonderful, multifaceted job filled with opportunity. No matter how you choose to carry out your mission, chances are you'll be forever influenced by the experience.

Local church communications is a ministry that shares the church's story in ways that move people toward becoming disciples for Christ. By being a local church communicator, you are following the ways of the Bible. In the following verses from Ephesians, include "communicator" (you) as one of the gifts to the church.

He is the one who gave gifts to the church: the apostles, the prophets, the evangelists, and the pastors and teachers. Their responsibility is to equip God's people to do his work and build up the church, the body of Christ, until we come to such unity in our faith and knowledge of God's Son that we will be mature and full grown in the Lord, measuring up to the full stature of Christ (Ephesians 4:11-13).

As a communicator, you are a storyteller and story listener, helping equip people with information, insight, and ways to respond in order to do God's work. You also provide the congregation with means to tell their own stories.

In Matthew 13:10 (*THE MESSAGE*), the disciples ask Jesus why he tells stories. He replied, "You've been given insight into God's kingdom. You know how it works. Not everybody has this gift, this insight; it hasn't been given to them. Whenever someone has a ready heart for this, the insights and understandings flow freely. But if there is no readiness, any trace of receptivity soon disappears. That's why I tell stories: to create readiness, to nudge the people toward receptive insight."

Think of the ways you as the communicator tell the story of the church, *creating readiness* and *nudging the church community toward receptive insight*. For example, you may help locate videos to put a face to people and ministries who benefit from the congregation's offerings, use the newsletter to connect Sunday school teachers with resources from the conference media center, publish personal stories on the website that entice individuals to get involved, coordinate banners on the church grounds to let the community know exciting things are happening, utilize social media tools to engage people and move the church toward being more welcoming, or coordinate revolving bulletin board information from ministries in the church. You provide vital links within the body of Christ!

Consider also how these passages apply to your ministry: *"He taught them by telling many stories" (Mark 4:2).* *"As she came in, the king was talking with Gehazi, the servant of the man of God. The king had just said, 'Tell me some stories about the great things Elisha has done' "* (2 Kings 8:4).

We have the greatest story of all to tell, and in this digital, multimedia world we have more options than ever before—and more challenges as a church to be relevant in telling our story in a way that inspires and engages people. That's why a communications coordinator is more important than ever!

Perhaps the goal of local church communications can be summed by Philippians 1:9, *"I pray that your love for each other will overflow more and more, and that you will keep on growing in your knowledge and understanding."*

Just as Mary was instructed to *"Go, tell"* when the tomb was empty, you are now asked to *"Go, tell."*

Understanding Your Role and Responsibilities

You are part of a leadership team that brings to life your church's vision and mission. Your role is to be a storyteller and connector, employing communications practices and tools to share the story of the church—its ministries, programs, opportunities, people, and faith—in planned, compelling, accessible ways. Your goal is to develop a reliable process for telling and hearing the church's story in which everyone can participate.

In its broadest sense, church communications is the sum total of everything we do, say, or show. Churches constantly communicate, whether they mean to or not. *Intentionally* communicating is the cornerstone of an effective communications ministry—and the essence of your job.

Your Role

Your hats may include what is known in the secular world as "marketing," "advertising," and "public relations," both inside the church and in the community.

As one local church communicator put it: communications ministry provides a way to take a large number of ministry events, needs, activities, and opportunities and package them for presentation to the congregation and the community.

You will want to interact frequently with the church council members. They are charged with coordinating programs of the church—elements of the church's story, in other words. They likely need your communications expertise. It will be helpful for you to read the other *Guidelines for Leading Your Congregation* in this series to learn more about everyone's jobs and to understand their communications needs.

Your Responsibilities

The ministry of communications encompasses such a wide and varied arena within the life of the church that it's difficult to identify exactly and accurately the responsibilities or resources for every communications coordinator. One size does not fit all. In general, the purpose of the communicator is to keep the congregation "in the know" about what's going on in the church and throughout the denomination and to challenge the congregation through stories of faith in action—bringing people closer in their walk with God.

It's important you sit with the pastor(s) and discuss your role and responsibilities so expectations are clear. One of the challenges communicators face is creating a manageable work life. There is so much to do! Let's look at a few areas that may be considered communications functions in the local church. One way to look at the tasks is to divide them according to complexity or responsibility.

Action Item: Use the following list as a discussion starter with your pastor and others about what fits your role, what others take care of, and where this position can go.

SUGGESTED BASIC RESPONSIBILITIES:

- Promote the church's mission through communications.
- Coordinate communications to and from members (print/electronic newsletters, announcements).
- Share information about members (bulletin boards, special recognitions).
- Promote church-related events and opportunities to church members to get their participation or involvement.
- Promote events and opportunities sponsored by the church to the community.
- Work with a communications committee.
- Make suggestions and contributions to the church's website.
- Utilize social media tools to create engagement, dialogue and community.

SUGGESTED INTERMEDIATE RESPONSIBILITIES (BUILDING ON THE BASICS):

- Provide creative communications counsel and direction for various ministries within the church as they organize and produce various events and services (e.g., identifying audiences, creating communications plans, sharing effective presentation ideas).
- Create a public relations plan for the church for both internal (congregation) and external (community) audiences.
- Write news releases and maintain proactive media relations.
- Write and design promotional and informational print materials.
- Ensure the church's building, property, and congregation communicates "welcome!" and promote good public relations.
- Coordinate "marketing" efforts of the church to support evangelism in reaching out to the community.
- Plan and place regular and seasonal advertising.
- Oversee the design and management of the church's Web ministry.

All these are "tasks." They are only as important as the reason behind doing them. Consider, what is the church's mission and vision? How does communication assist in breathing life into vision and mission statements?

NECESSARY SKILLS

Needed: Communications and organizational skills, sense of humor, ability to juggle several projects at once, a little patience, a love for The United Methodist Church and its people, a sense of mission, and an *occasional* ability to say no.

If you have been hired as the electronic communications coordinator, your work and tools will be different from the print person's, but your focus will be in sync with that of other communications staff.

In the Beginning

new coordinators of communication usually ask four basic questions:
1. What is my job?
2. Where do I begin?
3. How do we reach people in the congregation?
4. How do we make our church more visible in the community?

This Guideline will help you answer those questions, but it represents one toe in the water, just breaking the surface. If needed, you will want to tap additional resources for more in-depth discussion.

Where Do I Start?
1. Get clarity on the expectations of your position.
2. Learn about your annual conference.
3. Contact the conference director of communications, the district office, and other local church communicators.
4. Understand what you bring to the position and begin evolving the concept of what local church communications is for your local church.
5. Form a communications team.

You no doubt are already asking yourself, "What should communications for this church look like and how do I make it happen?" The answer will definitely evolve over time, but the question is a good motivator to launch a journey of discovery.

You know the adage, "It's not *what* you know, it's *who* you know"? That's a good place to start—finding the many "*who*" to support you along the way. The United Methodist Church is a connectional church, which means all United Methodist churches are connected in various ways—and help is available through the connection.

KNOW YOUR DISTRICT AND ANNUAL CONFERENCE
As a brief review, your local church is in a *district* within an *annual conference*. A district superintendent oversees several churches in the district. Get to know the superintendent and administrative person in your district office. They likely publish a newsletter and maintain a website. It's critical for you to have access to this information, as you may want to advertise and participate in district events and ministries, as well as promote your own local church events through the district. Ask to be on newsletter mailing lists—and ask how you can serve the communication needs of the district.

In the United States, an annual conference may include churches in one, part of one, or more than one state. Each annual conference is led by a bishop. There are nearly 60 annual conferences in the United States—the number changes as annual conferences merge. The number of churches in annual conferences range from 200 to more than 1,000. (There are about 70 annual conferences in Europe, Asia, and Africa.)

TAP INTO THE ANNUAL CONFERENCE

The annual conference office employs a staff that works with all aspects of ministry, including a director of communications. Early in your new position, call the director. (You should be able to obtain contact information from the conference website or from your pastor).

Ask the conference communicator what would be good for you to know as a new local church communicator: what programs and resources you should be aware of; what workshops might be available; what you can do to help the communicator; and so forth. This individual should be your go-to person and partner in ministry. When the conference is promoting ministry opportunities or sponsoring events, for example, he or she will count on you to help get the word out. Ask to be put on the conference newspaper and e-mail news lists. You also will want to look for stories in your church to be highlighted in conference news. Check the conference website and Facebook page often for ideas and resources.

Next, learn from others in similar positions. Ask the director if he or she knows of other local church communicators with whom you could visit. Don't be shy. Learning how others are walking the path is practical and will save you time and stress.

Action Item: Surf your annual conference's website. What ideas begin to bubble up?

GET ACQUAINTED WITH GENERAL AGENCIES

The annual conference is part of the general Church, as are 13 general boards and agencies. United Methodist Communications in Nashville, Tenn., is the denomination's official communications agency telling the church's story around the world. United Methodist Communications offers a variety of tools, services, training and resources that inform, inspire and engage local churches to reach their potential to carry out the mission of the church to make disciples of Jesus Christ for the transformation of the world.

> **Action Item:** Surf www.UMCom.org. Become familiar with how the website is organized and what it offers. Also look at the websites of other general agencies, such as the *General Board of Discipleship*, the *General Board of Global Ministries,* and *The United Methodist Publishing House*. You'll find resources to support many of your assignments.

As you see, you do not have to take this journey alone. While there is much to know, there is support. Just click or reach out and ask.

Build a Communications Team

You are terrific, but it's extremely difficult for one person alone effectively to vision, plan, implement, and evaluate local church communications. The strength of a team is the ability to brainstorm ideas one person could not think of alone and to spread the work and opportunity for serving among several persons.

Who should serve on the team? If the size and location of your congregation allows, include members on your committee who work or volunteer in areas of communication, such as writers, photographers, and specialists in electronic media or marketing/communications, public relations, and advertising. Include people new to the church.

Other helpful members include "idea persons" who represent the various age groups and who enjoy trying new strategies. It's important that youth and young adults have their own communications conversations and have a voice on the team. (See Guidelines for *Small Group Ministries* for ideas on working with your committee.)

After assembling your team, decide how often you will meet and for what reasons. Is this an advisory group or a working committee? If the team is a working group, empower the members to take on assignments, such as being reporters, writers, relationship-builders, or whatever their heart, head, and hands can do with passion and persistence.

The next order of business is to come to a common understanding of local church communications.

> **Action Item:** Give everyone a copy of this resource to read and discuss. In addition, you may want to invite a communicator from another congregation or from the annual conference office to visit and provide insights from his or her experiences.

Identifying Communications Needs

t o set you and your communications team on the road to success, you will be doing some start-up research. Where you begin depends on where you want to go. You need to know your destination so you can map your route. One way to find your destination is to ask this most important question of all:

"What do we want to happen or to be different as a result of having effective communications?"

Begin addressing this question by asking people in the church. Listen for their stories.

Ask church leaders. Spend time with the pastor, communications team, and church council to find out what they want to happen or to be different as a result of having effective communications. What are their communications visions and needs? What challenges does the church face that more effective communications would ease? What are their (and your) goals for more effective communication?

Make the goals concrete and *write them down.* Here are a few examples:

- We want 10 percent more of our congregation to be involved in hands-on mission work.

- We want to increase Special Sunday offerings by 5 percent.

- We would like the congregation and others to have access to daily devotional resources.

- We want to have our special services included on community calendars in newspaper and on radio.

By being specific, you will more effectively choose routes that will take you where you want to go and measure how well communications efforts are working. You soon will set priorities for addressing each of the goals.

Listen to the congregation. Now ask people in the congregation what information they want/need and how they want to receive it. What do they want/need to know about the church and its ministries (what will keep them in the "know"); what information will help them grow spiritually as disciples of Jesus Christ; and how and when do they want to receive the information? *Note:* Delivery preferences may be identified for different information needs, such as a letter from the pastor to catch attention versus a newsletter article for normal events.

You may survey the congregation by written/electronic questionnaires and listening sessions. Use one or both. Questionnaires can get to a large number of people. Listening sessions allow more in-depth discussions.

Encourage participation in information gathering with a note or statement from the pastor. It might read something like this:

> "We need your advice—and only *you* can help us. The church offers wonderful opportunities, but too many times we find out people don't know about them until it's too late. How can we do a better job of communicating?"

In the surveys, list the ways that you now communicate and ways you could possibly communicate in the future (probably additional digital avenues). Ask for their preferences and comments. Encourage them to identify at least three effective ways you can grab their attention.

Open-ended questions will capture rich ideas. Include questions such as: *"What do you need to hear or see that would catch your attention and add to your understanding?" "How can we communicate better with you?" "What helps you feel included in the community of the church?"*

Differences in age, background, and level of church involvement will affect their responses, so be sure to ask demographic questions (age, frequency of church attendance, church activities, and so forth).

Consider holding listening groups to glean preferences and new ideas. As a side benefit, people participating in these groups often are motivated to take an active role in creating solutions. Or, if you don't want to be this formal, just ask people what they think during normal conversation.

Be sure to include church leaders, such as Sunday school teachers, United Methodist Men and United Methodist Women, lay leaders, youth leaders, and, of course, the pastor(s) to find out what information/communications they need to do their jobs better.

Share findings among the communications team. This is where it gets fun. As a team, look at the results of the surveys and identify trends and patterns. Types of communications people want and need and the ways they prefer to receive and interact with it should emerge. Note differences in the demographics of responses. Are there trends? These will become your different audiences. (More on that later.) With experience and this information in hand, you and the team will become the experts in addressing your church's audiences and their communications needs.

Now, put the goals from leadership and the needs from the congregation together to create a plan. The plan will answer what, why, who, when, and how. From here on, the team will be involved in creating, implementing, and evaluating the plans.

Be sure to report survey results and plans for addressing them to leadership and to the congregation. Survey participants will appreciate the communication as confirmation of being partners in ministry.

Build Community

It's important to note communications is not just about providing information. An important role of communications is building community among the congregation and other persons associated with the church. A veteran local church communicator points out: *"People can only get involved if they know what's going on. Ministry and education are done in community, and communication is what creates and helps maintain that community."*

Effective communication makes people feel valued, important, cared for, and supported. It gives them connection—a sense of belonging, purpose, and commonality with others. Connection to meaningful experiences and relationships is a prime reason newcomers keep coming back! Being a valued member in a community of believers creates people who want to share and show the same love and caring to others. This is what John Wesley called a response to God's transforming grace in our lives.

Church is all about relationships. Use your tools in every way to build and strengthen those relationships. By employing the communication tools and techniques the congregation says it wants and needs, you will be able more effectively to focus on creating community.

Communication helps the congregation
1. grow spiritually.
2. be uplifted.
3. feel a part of the church community.
4. be active in the life of the church.
5. make informed decisions (about giving, for example).

Assessing Your Communications Tools

Once you have heard communications needs, it's a good time for you and the team to audit the communication tools your church currently uses or may plan to use. This is an effective way for team members to express their opinions and also their passion for communications.

Action Item: Break into pairs or small groups and assign the group a few of the tools until all the tools have been assigned. Report back and discuss in the large group. For each tool, identify:
1. Is it currently being used? If so,
2. How is it meeting identified needs?
3. For print and electronic pieces, are the look, feel, and message consistent? (Do all pieces contain the church logo, for example?)
4, How do you rate its effectiveness?
5. Should you keep it, improve it, or drop it?
6. If not in use, is it applicable in the future?

COMMUNICATIONS TOOLS AND RESOURCES

Announcement fliers
Audio/video streaming
Benevolence leaflets
Blogs
Brochures
Bulletin boards (electronic & other)
Bulletin inserts
Bumper stickers
Cable TV
Celebrations
Church directory
Church staff
Clothing w/church logo
Compact discs
Computers
Database
Direct mail
Discussion forums
Door hangers
DVDs

Newspaper ads
Online advertising
Outdoor advertising
Pamphlets
Personal visits
Photography/photo sharing
Podcasts
Posters
Pulpit announcements
Radio broadcasts
Radio spots
Room directories
Signs
Slogans
Special events
Table displays
Telephone
Television
Text messaging
Twitter

E-mail & e-newsletters
Face-to-face
Facebook
Fax machines
Handwritten notes
Invitational Sundays
Layout/design expertise
Letters
Logos
Multimedia
News releases
Newsletters

Themes or Phrases
Video productions
Videos/YouTube
Voicemail
Web-based discussion groups
Website
Welcome packets
Worship bulletins
Worship graphics
Yellow Pages
Others

Identify Foundational Communications

From your research, what will be the foundational ways to share information and build community through communications? For example, these may be electronic news updates, print newsletters, and website. What fits your situation?

Planning Ahead

i t's time to plan for the next 18 months. Doing "big picture" planning this far ahead assures that you will do the detailed planning soon enough to implement your plans. January may seem too early to make the detailed plans for a June vacation Bible school, but it isn't. Here's how:

Develop a Calendar

- With your pastor, church council chair, communications committee, and a large 18-month planning calendar, identify the important times and major events in the church year, including Special Sundays offering times. Mark those on the calendar. The United Methodist program calendar can help. If you're not certain of exact dates, indicate the month in which they are likely to happen.
- Determine if your publicity and companion stories need to center on one event (vacation Bible school) or multiple events and activities (Advent and Christmas season).
- Identify generally who will be the audiences you will want to reach and what tools you will want to use. Estimate what budget you will need—and plan how to fund it.
- Set a date to make your detailed plans and to begin to implement them. Note: Sometimes you will want to begin planning even before all of the details are finalized.
- Within a week or two following an event or season, evaluate your efforts—and begin planning for next year.

NEXT STEPS
Use the 18-month calendar information to develop an *overall* communications plan. Address the goals identified in your discussion with church leaders. Also, look for those times of the year when your church calendar is less full. Identify ministries and missions of the church about which you want people to know. Maybe you provide a food ministry to the community or offer enrichment activities for neighborhood children year around. Think about how you will build awareness and participation in the congregation and community. How about "Thanksgiving in June" to restock the food pantry? (This may be a good newspaper story because it has a "twist").

Action Item: With your team members, make a list of all the stories you would like to tell about the church (ministries, programs, people, and so forth). Decide how you will tell them best.

Create a Communications Plan

As you plan all the ways to communicate events and opportunities, keep in mind *"6 times, 3 ways."* Your research tells you how people say they will best respond, so find ways they will be exposed to the message six times in at least three different ways. You could tell them twice in the newsletter, one month on the bulletin board, six weeks on a banner, as well as through personal contact/presentation, phone call, or bulletin insert. And put everything on the website, if you have one.

Plan ways that not only tell but also show and allow hands-on experiences. Engage all your audience's senses—sight, sound, touch, even smell in some cases! Update your plan at least quarterly.

Sample Communications Plan Outline
Here's an outline of a communications plan. Use it for single events or activities. Adapt it to present your full communications plan.

I. Objective
What do we want to accomplish? (Keep in mind how it advances the church's vision and mission.)

II. Communications
    A. What is our message? (Force yourself to write this in one sentence!)
    B. Who is the target audience/audiences?
    C. What three (or more) tools or media will best reach the audience?
    D. How will we deliver the message so people see it six times?
    E. What communications barriers can we anticipate, and how will we overcome them?

III. Implementation
    A. Who will coordinate and monitor this communications plan?
    B. What is our timeline for implementing each part of the plan?
    C. Who is responsible for each task?
    D. Where are the checkpoints to be certain the plan is working?

IV. Budget
What will be the cost? Consider finances, time, volunteers.

V. Evaluation
    A. How will we assess what we did?
    B. Is immediate follow-up needed?
    C. What will we do differently next time?

Once you do this a few times, it will flow easily—and be worth every minute!

Set Priorities

Set priorities on communications. Start where you are and build as you can. Take a little at a time. For example, what will be the four primary ways of communicating with members? Work toward making those tools more effective.

Outline your primary communications approaches. Here is an example:

Communicating with the congregation
- Weekly e-mail updates
- Face-to-face sharing: setting aside time during the church service for personal stories of outreach, and so forth
- Newly designed worship bulletin that contains information about classes and opportunities to serve and be in lay ministry
- Start or expand a church Facebook page

Communicating with the community
- Weekly advertisement in the newspaper
- Upcoming events in community calendars
- Monthly news releases about special people, ministries, or community involvement

Welcoming guests and visitors
- Brochure and video about the church
- Newcomer packet with church brochure, Q&A sheet, bookmark or magnet with a memorable message *"Brought to you* by _____"
- Improved "body language" of the church building and grounds
- Welcoming training for the congregation

Strategic public relations
- Participation in community-wide events (parades, special observances)
- Offer classes to meet the needs of the neighborhood or community (You can ask what they need. Residents of one neighborhood said they needed to know about pest control, so that's what the church provided.)

Internal and external audiences
- Website evaluation and update

Create the Tie That Binds

No matter what tools you decide to use, strive for a consistent look and feel for all print and electronic materials. Use a logo and slogan on business cards (for laity as well as clergy), letterhead, brochures, newsletters, fliers, and website.

Consider using the denomination's promise: *"Open hearts. Open doors. Open minds. The people of The United Methodist Church."* Local churches are using it to tie everything together by making it visible everywhere, including wearing it on clothing during special events. By using this for your local church, you are joining the identity of churches around the world and plugging into a recognizable image—and, at the same time, building pride and a sense of belonging among members. But use it *only* if it's true for your congregation—that everyone is an honored guest and welcome. Welcoming training is available through United Methodist Communications. Talk with your conference communicator about opportunities.

The rest of this resource will highlight information that will provide support for developing your communications plans.

Know Your Audiences

Your audience has a tremendous influence on *what* to say, *how* to say it, *when* to say it, *where* to say it, and *who* should say it. Particularly in a communications campaign, you will want and *need* to identify audiences to target. You can do this in several ways, including by family life-cycle groups (unmarried, newly married, full nest, empty nest); by generation; by lifestyle. Within each group are subgroups. For singles, there are older adult singles, divorced singles, widowed, and so on. Consider these differences as you develop your messages and plans.

Selecting the Right Vehicle

i f your communications plan is a road map, what vehicles will you use to get to you destination? The next several pages outline various options.

The Church Newsletter

A good newsletter can be one of the most effective tools for your church or ministry. A print newsletter is seen by far more people than those who hear the weekly sermon, and it can be a great vehicle for advancing your church's vision and mission. Conversely, a poor-quality newsletter can have a negative or embarrassing effect.

Many local churches use both print and electronic newsletters—and put them on the website after they're sent. Electronic newsletters can be created in the body of an e-mail or can use HTML formatting. HTML creates the ability to add color, font styles, and layout. They make it simple to send timely messages to your entire church or targeted messages to specific groups, such as worship leaders, ushers or Sunday school teachers. Newsletters can direct readers to the website for additional information.

WHY PUBLISH A NEWSLETTER?

The purpose of the church newsletter should be to *educate, inform,* and, most of all, *to boost and sustain congregational morale*—a key ingredient in community building.

Boosting morale means including stories that make the church stand out in the community, such as about how much is raised in the CROP walk compared to the rest of the community. It also means explaining issues affecting the church, such as new construction or receiving a new pastor, and addressing readers' questions and concerns. Listen to questions you hear the congregation asking. Reflect on people's needs identified earlier in these Guidelines. Think about how to create content that meets those needs.

Newsletters (and website) stories can include new member profiles, issues, activities, interpretations of numbers and actions, and information about the structure and polity of the denomination. In the stories, answer for the reader, *"How does this affect me?"* or *"What does it mean?"* Use the newsletter to stimulate interest in service and ministry by highlighting the opportunities and by putting a face to those opportunities through readers' real-life experiences. Remember, you are a storyteller.

Readers will look for names of people they know. Highlight a volunteer or member each month. Let their story of service and faith walk encourage others. Use photographs! They capture interest and tell the story.

A calendar of events is especially helpful. Short summaries of general church news from UMC.org and United Methodist News Service and of district or conference news help to keep people involved with our connectional system. Conduct readership surveys every 18 months to learn what people want and don't want.

WHO IS THE NEWSLETTER AUDIENCE?

The primary audience for the newsletter is the congregation. Beyond that, the newsletter can serve as a news source and public relations tool. You may choose to send it to guests and visitors, media representatives, other clergy, district and conference communicators, members in the armed services, missionaries, college students, former members who have moved away, people who have participated in or contributed to the church or its ministry, and medical offices and other places with waiting rooms.

TIPS FOR GETTING YOUR NEWSLETTER READ

- Find an attractive format. You may want to use a template that is part of your word processing program. The newsletter style you select portrays an image of the church: traditional, contemporary, and so forth.

- Twelve-point type for body copy is comfortable for most readers. Headlines should be larger and in boldface, and should create interest in the story.

- A 2- or 3-column format works best. The ideal line has 7 or 8 words, between 40 and 50 characters.

- Put the most important story on the top of page one under the nameplate. Discourage the pastor from putting his or her column here.

- Write stories that give a "face" to the church and its ministries.

- Write about what's coming up, not so much about what's already happened.

- Remember the readers who will only glance at the newsletter for 30 seconds. What will catch their attention?

- Use standing columns for which people will look each time.

- Highlight members' names in bold.

- Remember to include who, what, when, where, why, and how in all stories.

- Recruit others to edit and proofread.

TIPS FOR EFFECTIVE E-NEWSLETTERS

- Always offer recipients the option to subscribe or unsubscribe.

- Create a subject line that identifies your church or ministry e-newsletter and then lists the theme of the e-newsletter or the lead article.

- Keep it short (just like the average web surfer's attention span). Your articles should be concise. If you want to include more information or expand an idea, simply link to a website.

- Create a table of contents at the top of the e-newsletter to help your readers navigate and easily locate articles they want to read.

- Keep it consistent. Follow the same template each time to brand your church's e-newsletter and help readers easily identify your mission.

- Enhance articles with a photo, but don't go overboard. If you want to display an entire photo album, post them on your Facebook page or website and just create a link.

- Create a plain text version of your e-newsletter for recipients who can only receive your e-newsletter in plain text. Most e-mail service providers have this feature built in so that you can create an all-text version with minimal effort.

- Set a delivery schedule. Send e-newsletters at least once a month to keep the lines of communication open.

- Always provide your church's physical address, phone number, and links to your website and social media pages. Group these elements in the same place of each e-newsletter for easy reference.

E-mail

E-mail can keep the congregation connected in ways we once thought impossible. E-mail provides a wonderful opportunity to share news on short notice, such as illness, deaths, or job openings, promote your church, publicize activities and grow your ministry with little to no cost. Save trees and save money!

Electronic news lists enable you to segment your audiences easily. Growing your ministry is as simple as hitting forward. People are more likely to spread your message with the forward button on their e-mail account than share something they read on paper. This will increase your church's exposure and keep your members informed.

Just follow these quick tips, and remember to always proofread for spelling and grammatical errors:

- Typically, choose e-mail (as opposed to an e-newsletter) when communicating with an individual or a small group.

- Send messages from an e-mail account that uses the name of your church or ministry, not the name of an individual.

- Use the BCC field to contact groups. This ensures recipients' privacy and keeps them happy if they haven't given you permission to share their e-mail addresses.

- Avoid adding large attachments. Put everything in the body of the e-mail or create links to additional information on the web.

- To pique readers' interest, make sure subject lines and messages are concise and relevant. This will make them more likely to open and read future messages from you.

- Aim to keep subject lines between 25 and 50 characters.

- Promote your church with an e-mail signature. Most e-mail applications allow you to create a signature to insert automatically each time you send out a message. In the signature, include any pertinent contact information with links to your website and/or social media pages.

- Consistently check and respond to incoming e-mail messages to keep the lines of communication open.

• Regularly keep track of e-mail address changes and immediately delete contacts who ask to be removed from your list.

Church Brochures

Your church may have several brochures. Each must have a particular purpose (such as highlighting one ministry) and carry out that purpose by combining form, design, content, and language to communicate effectively. Yet, each should look like it's in the same church family of design.

A basic publicity brochure about the church is especially useful for distribution to new and prospective members. It summarizes the congregation's purposes, ministries, services, and so on. When designing the brochure, keep in mind, *"Why would someone be interested in this church?"*

Use good quality paper, interesting pictures, compelling graphics, an attractive layout, and succinct, well-written copy. Keep the brochure focused and simple. Assume the reader knows nothing about your program or ministry. Use language the reader understands (remember *audience*). Focus on the human element, and don't be afraid to use "you." If possible, use design elements that tie it to the website.

WAYS TO USE CHURCH BROCHURES

Make available in high-traffic areas in the church; mail to neighbors; supply to area realtors; include in the visitor's packet; supply to the local chamber of commerce; send to other ministers; include in a media or press kit; display in area hotels, motels, and transportation terminals.

Website & Web Ministry

With the prevalence of the Internet, church members and seekers increasingly expect churches to have a web presence—both for basic information and as a tool for evangelism. You can minister to a congregation that's even larger than your surrounding community by maintaining a website and creating a web ministry.

You will also want to check your church's listing on the online denominational directory at www.UMC.org/find-a-church. It's easy to update your listing anytime right on the site.

BUILDING A WEBSITE

Many seekers look at a church's website before they decide to visit. It allows those searching for a church to learn more about it before committing to a visit. Here are a few things to consider when building a website:

- Consider the initial purpose and mission of the site. Will you be sharing news and information? Using it as a ministry? Introducing the church?

- Think about your primary audience. Are you targeting church members? Web surfers? Church seekers?

- Visit other local church websites to get ideas for your own. Evaluate what you like about their sites and what you would do differently.

- What is the budget for your website? Consider using online courses and resources to get your website up and running (available at www.umcom.org/training).

- Designate someone to design the site, administer and maintain it.

- Include the following foundational sections: about us, theological background of your church, worship and regular event times, current events, directions to the church, profiles of your pastor(s) and staff, program/ministry descriptions, and basic contact info.

- Provide links to related sites where viewers can get additional information about your activities and The United Methodist Church.

CREATING A WEB MINISTRY

Having a website is just part of growing a dynamic, interactive web ministry. Web ministry offers avenues of timely, critical response and engagement with members and seekers across the world and helps you connect with billions of web users 24 hours a day, 7 days a week, 365 days a year. Web ministry adapts the unparalleled tools of the Internet to fulfill the church's mission of making disciples of Jesus Christ for the transformation of the world.

Consider these quick tips for establishing your church's web ministry:

- Form a team of at least three people who have a passion for using technology as a ministry tool.

- Secure buy-in from key people and groups to ensure everyone is onboard with your web ministry plans and is prepared to assist, as needed, to keep the ministry alive.

- Develop a purpose and goals for your ministry that align with your church's overall mission.

- Identify your ministry's target audience and get to know what they expect and need from your online presence.

- Create a podcast. Post weekly sermons or special presentations.

- Consider taking the online web ministry course for step-by-step guidance in using Internet tools for ministry at www.umcom.org/training.

- Establishing a presence on the web helps your church be accessible, current, accurate, quick, and comprehensive. Show the world how God is at work in your church.

Social Media

Social media tools such as Facebook, Twitter, and YouTube are great ways to engage your congregation and help members stay connected between worship services and other church events. It's also a good way to increase visibility of your church and make information available to members, seekers, and visitors for little to no cost.

Used effectively, social media can create engagement, dialogue, and community so that communication is no longer one-way. You're not just passing along information, but creating conversation and connecting people with one another.

Aim for a good mix of content. You can share photos, post events, create discussion groups, pose conversation starters, ask for feedback—in short, get to know one another. You can also post links to stories that are relevant to your congregation, whether related to your local community or the larger global church.

A good place to begin is www.umcom.org/socialmedia. There you will find a wealth of information about social media strategies and how to use them for ministry.

Videos

Making messages come alive through video can be an effective approach to telling the church's story and putting a face on ministries and programs. Videos have the advantage of creating images through sight and sound. They can take a person on location and create a mood or an intended emotional response.

One word of caution: videos/DVDs made for young people need the guidance of a professional or someone who understands the pacing, pictures, music, and graphics necessary to keep a video interesting for the digital media generation.

Before planning to make a video, consider this important point: Does the subject matter lend itself to a video format? That is, can the pictures tell the story? Talking heads are not a good use of your video resources. Video is the medium of action.

Use a story format. For example, if your goal is to explain where apportionment dollars are spent, you might focus on the story of an individual who has benefited from a project made possible by apportionments.

Be mindful of the needs of your audience. Your goal should be to connect the audience to your message: to reinforce their thinking, inform them, make them feel good about the ministries and want to take action.

UMTV offers compelling video stories of United Methodist church members and ministries changing the world today. Churches can use these features in worship services, Sunday school classes, and other group settings.

Go Multimedia

Remember "6 times, 3 ways"? Multimedia can help. Let's say you want to tell the story of a mission trip to encourage others to participate. Write a story for the print newsletter and one for the web, where you can add pictures and comments from participants, plus a short video clip. Reference the web story in the newsletter. Put a blurb in the electronic newsletter (maybe even a teaser for an upcoming newsletter story) and link to the web story. Show the video during coffee time or in the narthex. See how this ties your media together, increases visibility, and says, "Hey, this is important!"

Interpreting Connectional Giving

*W*hat one cannot do alone, we can do together. You and the other members of your church are part of a worldwide ministry of love and care. Every congregation supports that ministry through apportioned funds, Special Sundays, and The Advance for Christ and His Church. We call this "connectional giving." Congregations are enriched by regular communications about United Methodism's amazing missions connection and how it is funded.

Telling about these ministries and promoting the fair-share support of the benevolence funds is an important task of your congregation's leadership team. As communications coordinator, you can locate stories and resources and suggest strategies to communicate effectively. Fortunately, materials and people can help.

- See your pastor first. Materials describing the work of the wider church are sent to the pastor's office regularly. Pastors can pinpoint people and resources within your congregation as well as in your region. To order your own set of materials, or to order in quantity for your congregation (shipped to you at no expense to your local church), call United Methodist Communications customer support at 1-888-346-3862. There are many resources online to help you with promoting the support of the mission of the global church.

- Learn more about connectional giving through the free online course offered at www.umcom.org/training. In just a few hours, you and members of your church can work through an engaging tour of how connectional giving and connectional living distinguish us as United Methodists.

- Talk with leaders responsible for missions and United Methodist Women. They may know regional resource leaders who can provide ideas and stories.

- Your conference newspaper is an ongoing source of information.

- Check with your conference resource center, treasurer, or district office for printed and audiovisual resources that will help with interpretation and promotion.

- *The Official Program Calendar of The United Methodist Church* is an excellent source of information about funds, offerings, and other observances.

- Throughout the quadrennium, your annual conference and the general church provide new materials to promote and interpret conference and general church funds. Many can be ordered by calling 888-346-3862.

- The Special Sundays highlight key ministries. Work with your pastor to schedule these observances. Materials are available to interpret each observance.

Be creative and have fun sharing the stories and connecting your congregation with our church at work around the world.

Action Item:
Explore www.umcgiving.org to learn more about connectional giving and resources to make your assignment easier.

Projecting a Positive Image

Projecting a positive image is important both to your existing congregation and to the community.

Create Visibility in the Community

How do you get people in the community to notice you? You become more visible through invitation, public witness, word-of-mouth, advertising, and good public relations. While publicity about activities is certainly a key element in attracting attention, so are new and exciting programs and ministries that meet the needs of the community and have people talking.

Public Witness as Public Relations

Public relations is a communications tool that seeks to influence attitudes in order to gain support. Church public relations are affected by the way your church handles its reputation and image, based upon its witness. Through outreach ministries, you can demonstrate to the world that faith in Christ is active and that church is not a place, but rather a way of life. That's communication! It tells a story about your church.

Body Language as Public Relations

Congregational communication is not limited to verbal and printed messages. Churches exude a kind of body language that may either reinforce or contradict their other messages. Churches that proclaim, "All are welcome" but ignore visitors are guilty of false advertising at the very least.

Some of the most eloquent messages from your church are unspoken. The church building, the grounds, and the sign are on view 24 hours a day. All of them send out silent signals that may affect the way your church is perceived. As a key player on the communication team, it may be your responsibility to see that everything connected to your church carries out its vision and mission in a positive way.

The saying, "You only have one chance to make a good first impression" might have been coined for church communications. Studies have shown that visitors make up their minds in the *first 11 minutes* whether or not they're coming back to a church. That time is usually spent finding a parking place, locating the proper entrance, being greeted, and finding a seat. No matter how eloquent the sermon, the opinion of a visitor is often shaped by unspoken messages long before the service begins!

BODY LANGUAGE TIPS:

The *church sign* should be at right angles to the street in front of the build-ing, visible to people driving in both directions. It should be seen easily from the far lane with letters large enough to be read from a moving car. Include worship times—and if those times change on a particular Sunday, be sure to change them on the sign. Don't underestimate the invitation value of your sign!

The *church grounds* should reflect cleanliness, order, and harmony. Good landscaping, neatly trimmed grass, and an absence of leaves and litter indi-cate a high level of pride. We hear stories of people deciding to attend a church because of how neatly the church grounds are maintained. Clearly mark buildings and doors so a visitor will know which place to enter.

Make sure the *church entrance* is well lighted and inviting. Mark bath-rooms clearly, and place directional signs in the foyer leading to the nursery and the church office.

Bulletin boards may be one of the first things a person notices inside the church. Your board should convey a positive image of the church and connect church members to it. It should evolve constantly to reflect the changing dynamics of church life. If it doesn't change, people quit look-ing at it.

Telephones as Public Relations

Telephones provide personal contact and are seen as a reflection of the church. A caller will decide in the first few moments of contact whether your faith community is friendly, professional, and reliable. *Voice mail* may be the first point of contact with your church, so it is an important ele-ment in successful communications. After hours, the voice on your answer-ing machine should be cheerful, enthusiastic, and friendly. Especially on weekends, your recorded message should include the church address and times of the services, and a number for emergencies, *but little more*. Invite the caller to leave a detailed message and make sure all calls are returned promptly.

Welcoming as Public Relations

As prospective new members, visitors are a transfusion into the lifeblood of the church. If your communications evangelism brought the visitors to the church, then they are your invited guests. Congregations are discovering how important it is to be intentionally inviting and develop a welcoming lifestyle.

Assist Persons with Special Needs

Integral in being welcoming is providing accessibility for those with limiting physical conditions. With an aging population, it's a benefit worth promoting.

Include the accessibility logo in ads and posters. Provide clear directions to accessible entrances. Advertise services with deaf interpretation.

Media Ministry: Sending the Word

i s your church ready to start spreading the word about your local ministries, but unsure how to get started? Here are three ways to jump-start your media efforts with a limited budget:

Build on the foundation of The United Methodist Church's national advertising. The United Methodist Church maintains a national advertising presence throughout the year. Research indicates that people who are not currently involved in church are receptive to spiritual messages during Lent (the weeks before Easter), back-to-school (August-September) and Advent (right before Christmas). The United Methodist Church places national television advertising during these special events, as well as during times of disaster to provide messages of hope and help. For more information, contact your conference communicators and visit umcom.org/rethinkchurch.

Create a targeted media presence with Rethink Church. Go beyond your church's walls to serve your community with the Rethink Church initiative. Rethink Church provides creative elements throughout the year to help local churches build a media presence. Media buys through Rethink Church are more targeted and customized to specific audiences for more effective messaging. For more information, visit www.umcom.org/rethinkchurch.

Send out news releases about your ministries. Include the most important information in the first paragraph. Don't forget the basics. Include who, what, when, where, why and how. Make it easy for the person receiving the release to catch the most important information with just a quick read-through. Follow up with contacts at media outlets to make sure they received the release, and make yourself available to answer any questions.

CHURCH STORY POSSIBILITIES FOR MEDIA ATTENTION

- New staff members in key positions
- Notable guests

- Outstanding volunteers
- Responses to disasters
- Unique or new programs or approaches
- Community initiatives and events
- Record-breaking or award-winning projects
- Travel by congregation members involving a special activity
- Participation by staff or members in national or international meetings
- Construction/remodeling, both beginning and completion
- Local angles to national religious stories

Maintain Good Media Relations

Learn to work effectively with the local media. Get to know the religion writer of the daily paper, the news directors at popular radio stations, the editor of the local weekly newspaper and other reporters who cover the type of stories you are promoting and build good working relationships with them. Learn about their needs, deadlines, and policies; what they consider newsworthy; and what kinds of stories run most often.

Compile a list of names of reporters, editors, and news directors, along with their phone and fax numbers and e-mail addresses if possible. Be sure that the names are accurately spelled, and update your list regularly.

Reporters are not interested in giving publicity to people and churches. They are looking for news stories that interest people. You can help them find those stories. Frame your story in such a way that shows why it is significant for the local community and how it impacts people outside the church. In other words, consider your audience and ask yourself how this news relates to them. Don't wear out your welcome with the media by sending what news reporters consider mundane stories about the church bake sale or the Wednesday night potluck.

Television stations will be more interested in reporting your story if it has a creative or unique visual element. An event or activity that is out-of-the-ordinary is more apt to attract television cameras. When sending a news release to a print publication, include a high-quality photo if appropriate. The more distinctive or original the photo, the more likely it is to be used.

Once you've established a relationship, ask all your media contacts if they want to be put on your church mailing list to receive the newsletter and other special mailings. Don't send them unless they ask. *Update your media contact list frequently.*

Explore the Media

Church advertising is an effective way to promote your congregation's message to your community—whether through print, radio, television, billboards, cinema ads, or online.

Placing church TV ads is a great way to reach out visually to seekers. Television conveys emotions and images that reflect the message you are trying to communicate. When broadcast television is unaffordable or unavailable, local cable television may be an option.

If you know who you want to reach with your message, **radio** can be a good choice because they have demographic information that will help you find your target audience. Radio stations have a clear idea of their audience because stations shape programming to attract certain types of listeners, and offer specialized formats such as "adult contemporary," "rock," "talk," and so forth. **Don't choose radio, however, if your church is far from the metropolitan area where a station is located, because you may be spending money on messages to an audience who will most likely not attend your church because of distance.**

The more often you can get a spot or program aired, the more effective it will be. Churches have more success on radio and **cable TV** when they place 26 ads in a two-day time span rather than 26 ads in a seven-day time span.

Daily newspapers reach a broad audience, but newspaper readers tend to be older. Ad placement in the paper is critical. People are most likely to notice an ad in the upper-right hand column on an odd-numbered page toward the front of the paper. If your target audience is unchurched people, put your ad in the sports, business, or classified section. If you're trying to attract someone looking for a church, put your ad in the religion section. Newspaper advertising rates vary significantly from day to day, and many newspapers offer package deals.

Community newspapers are circulated in and focus upon a smaller area. They are generally published weekly, which gives them a longer "shelf life" than dailies. Their rates are less than daily newspapers, and they tend to be more receptive to stories about churches in the area.

Shopper papers and others that are free may provide good coverage, but as a rule, they are not taken as seriously as subscription papers. Your message may get lost among all the other ads.

Billboards can be effective depending on their location. The more desirable the location, the more expensive they can be. Use no more than seven words of copy with professionally done artwork. Ads must be eye-catching and easily understood from a moving automobile.

Direct mail can be sent exactly where you want it to go. Mailings for church events are best when sent six to eight weeks before the event. Connect your direct mail pieces with a unifying theme and distinctive "look." The key to success in direct mail advertising is developing a good mailing list and including a response form with clear instructions for the intended result. Address lists can be purchased from direct-mail companies. Call them and discuss options.

Classified display ads in the Yellow Pages often reach newcomers to town and others looking for a church to attend.

Bumper stickers and clothing, if professionally designed, can provide a traveling advertisement for your church. Keep your message simple.

Prospective church members may search for a greater spiritual presence **online** or participate in other online activities. You can reach various audience segments with a well-thought strategic approach to online advertising.

United Methodist Communications can assist you with media planning and buying to ensure your church obtains the most efficient advertising buy possible. Media services are provided at no cost to any local United Methodist church. A variety of free customizable advertising resources are also available. For more information, call (877) 281-6535 or e-mail Rethinkchurch.org@umcom.org.

Venturing Forth

Action Item: Have committee members identify three things they found the most important or useful in the *Guidelines for Communications*. Discuss: How will the committee put those things in place?

You're not alone in your work. You have your conference director of communications, United Methodist Communications, and a host of colleagues throughout the connection. Of special interest may be membership and attendance at the United Methodist Association of Communicators (UMAC) events. You will meet communicators from around the world at the annual meeting. For more information, talk with your conference communicator and go to www.umcommunicators.org. Contact United Methodist Communications in Nashville, Tennessee at 1-888-278-4862 to let them know you are a local church communicator and want to participate in the life of United Methodist Communications.

Thank you for your work. Know that most church communicators pray for patience, more help, and more hours in the day. Be blessed as you select the most important things you can do. Godspeed.

Here's expert advice from a local church communicator:
First and always, pray about your calling.
Second, keep a sense of humor. Somebody always wants something at the last minute.
Third, accept that you will never get everything done. Just do your best— and pray some more.

Resources

Official website of The United Methodist Church: www.umc.org

InfoServ, United Methodist Information Service: www.infoserv.umc.org

United Methodist Communications (UMCom) www.umcom.org.
  Communications agency for The United Methodist Church.
Advertising plan for a local church: Call 877-281-6535, or e-mail
  Rethinkchurch@umcom.org
Customer service: 888-346-3862 or e-mail csc@umcom.org
Local church marketing: www.umcom.org/churchmarketing
Local church communication audit resources: www.umcom.org/ccresources
Find-A-Church online directory: www.find-a-church.org
Welcoming ministry: www.umcom.org/welcoming
Web ministry: www.umcom.org/webministry
Connectional Giving: www.umcgiving.org
Rethink Church/Change the World: www.umcom.org/rethinkchurch
Rethink Church events (advertising grants): www.umcom.org/impactcom
  munity
Social media ministry: www.umcom.org/socialmedia
Communications training: www.umcom.org/training
MyCom (communications e-newsletter): www.umcom.org/mycom
TechShop (discount hardware, software, and Web solutions):
  www.umcom.org/techshop

PUBLICATIONS
Interpreter (United Methodist Communications): www.interpreter
  magazine.org.
  Official ministry magazine of The United Methodist Church

Official United Methodist Program Calendar (United Methodist
  Communications).
  Call 888-346-3862 or order online at www.umcom.org/store.

Speaking Faith: The Essential Handbook for Religion Communicators
  (Religion Communications Council (RCC).
  Order at www.religioncommunicators.org.

The Church Communications Handbook, by Wanda Vasallo (Kregel
  Publishing, 1998). ISBN 978-0825-43925-4. A comprehensive look at
  local church communications. Available at www.cokesbury.com.

Web-Empower Your Church: *Unleashing the Power of Internet Ministry* (Abingdon Press, 2006). ISBN: 978-0-68764-284-7. Available at www.cokesbury.com.

Reaching Out in a Networked World: *Expressing Your Congregation's Heart and Soul* by Lynne M. Baab (Alban Institute, 2008). ISBN 978-1-56699-368-5. Available at www.alban.org.

Getting the Word Out: *The Alban Guide to Church Communications* by Frederick H. Gonnerman (Alban Institute, 2003). ISBN 1-56699-283-4. Available at www.alban.org.

Healthy Discourse: *Solving Communication Quandaries in Congregations* by Kibbie Simmons Ruth and Karen A. McClintock (Alban Institute, 2007). ISBN 978-1-56699-346-3. Available at www.alban.org.

ARTICLES
"Cleaning Up Bad Communication Habits"
http://www.alban.org/conversation.aspx?id=6138

"Speaking the Truth in Love"
http://www.alban.org/conversation.aspx?id=5042

UNITED METHODIST NEWS RESOURCES
United Methodist News Service (news, videos, commentaries):
www.umns.umc.org

Graphics Library and Photo Galleries: www.umc.org/graphicslibrary

Newscope (concise, late-deadline weekly news update):
www.umph.com/newscope

News in Pews (newsletter template): www.umc.org/newsinpews

UMR Communications: www.umr.org

UMTV (video stories about people making a difference): www.umtv.org

ORGANIZATION
United Methodist Association of Communicators (UMAC):
www.umcommunicators.org

NOTES

_____

_____

_____

_____

_____

_____

_____

_____

_____

_____

_____

_____

_____

_____

_____

_____

_____

_____

_____

_____

_____

_____

NOTES

NOTES

NOTES

NOTES

GUIDELINES FOR LEADING YOUR CONGREGATION

NOTES

NOTES